LITTLE RED RIDING HOOD COLORING BOOK

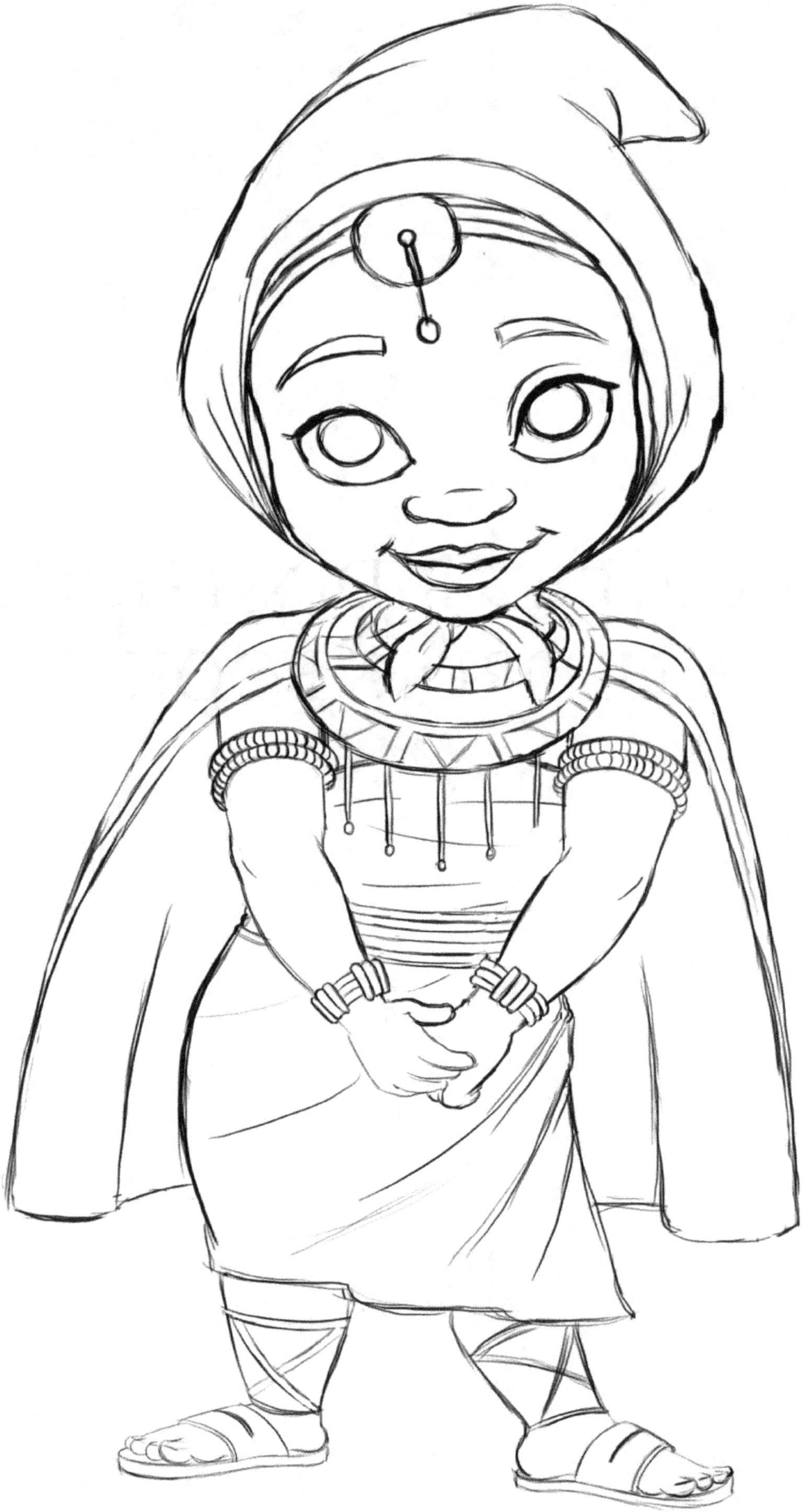

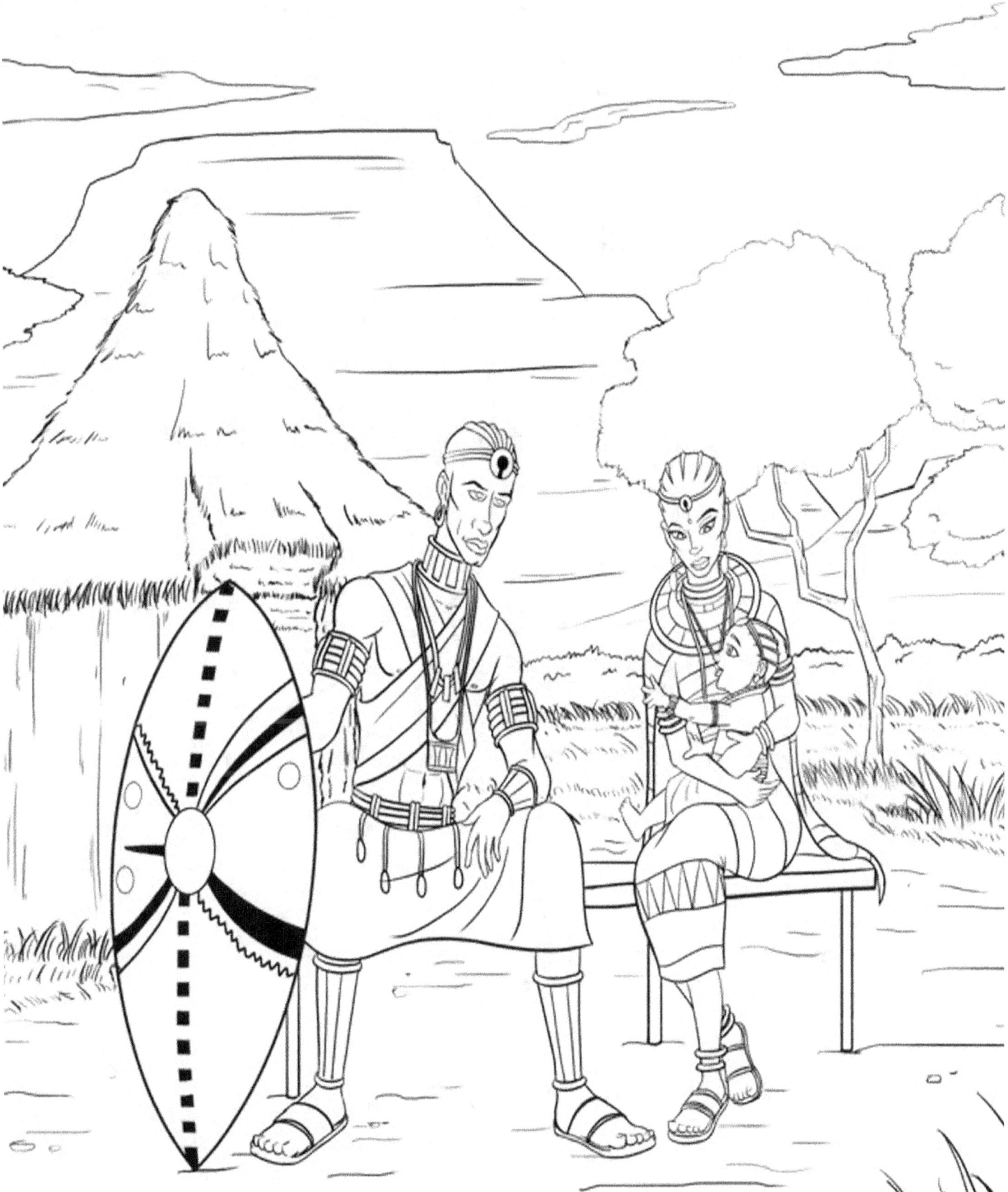

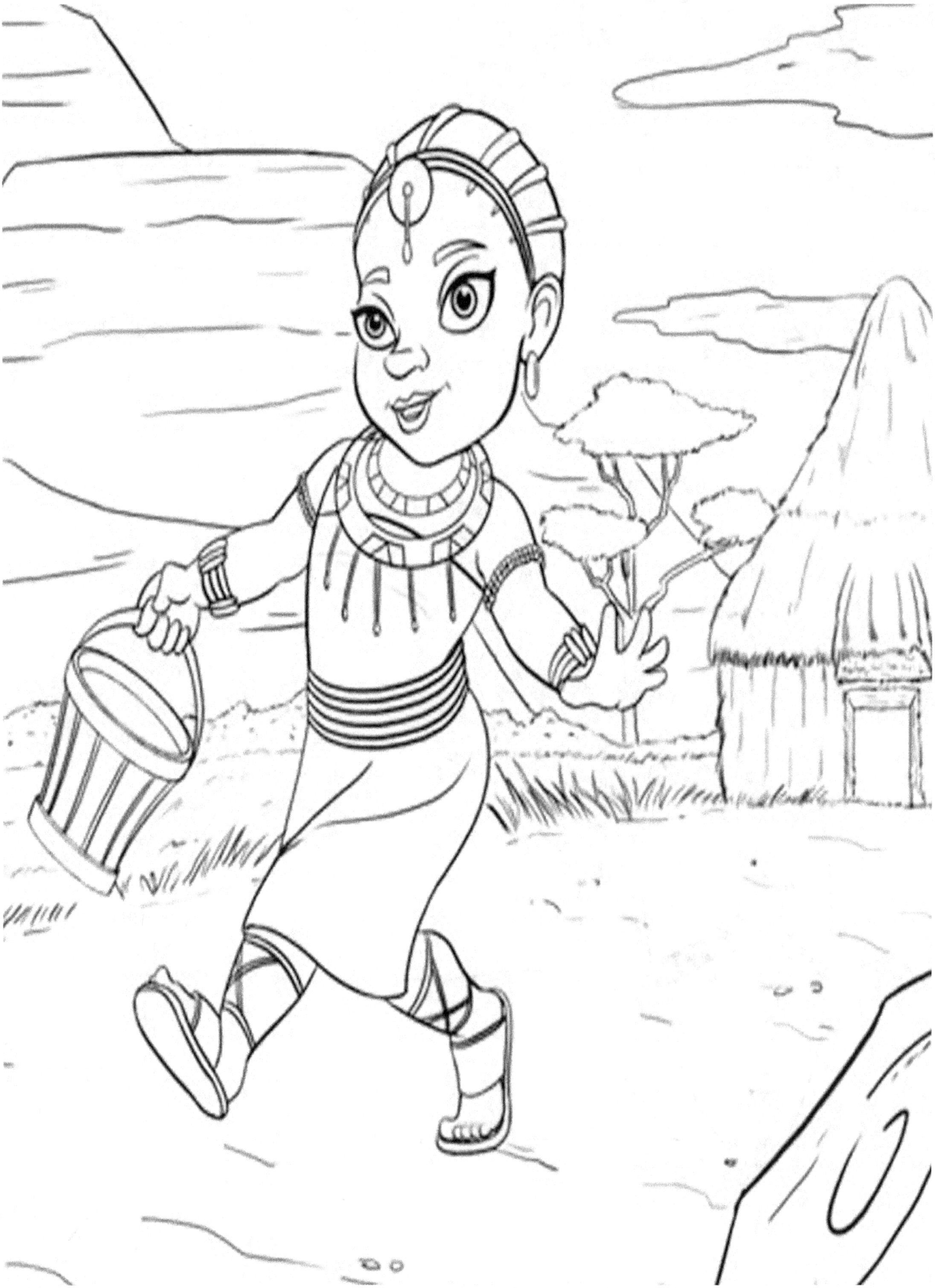

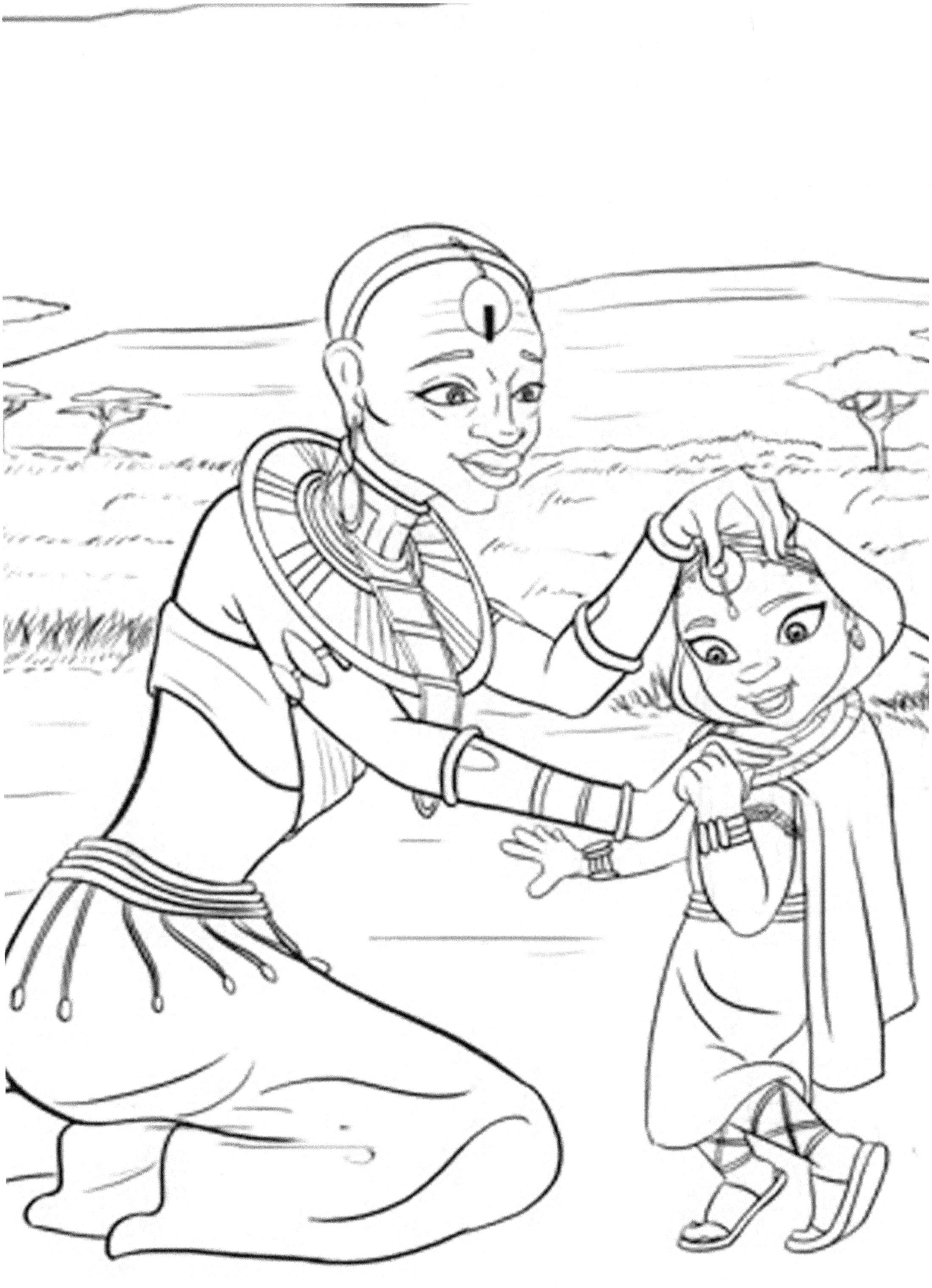

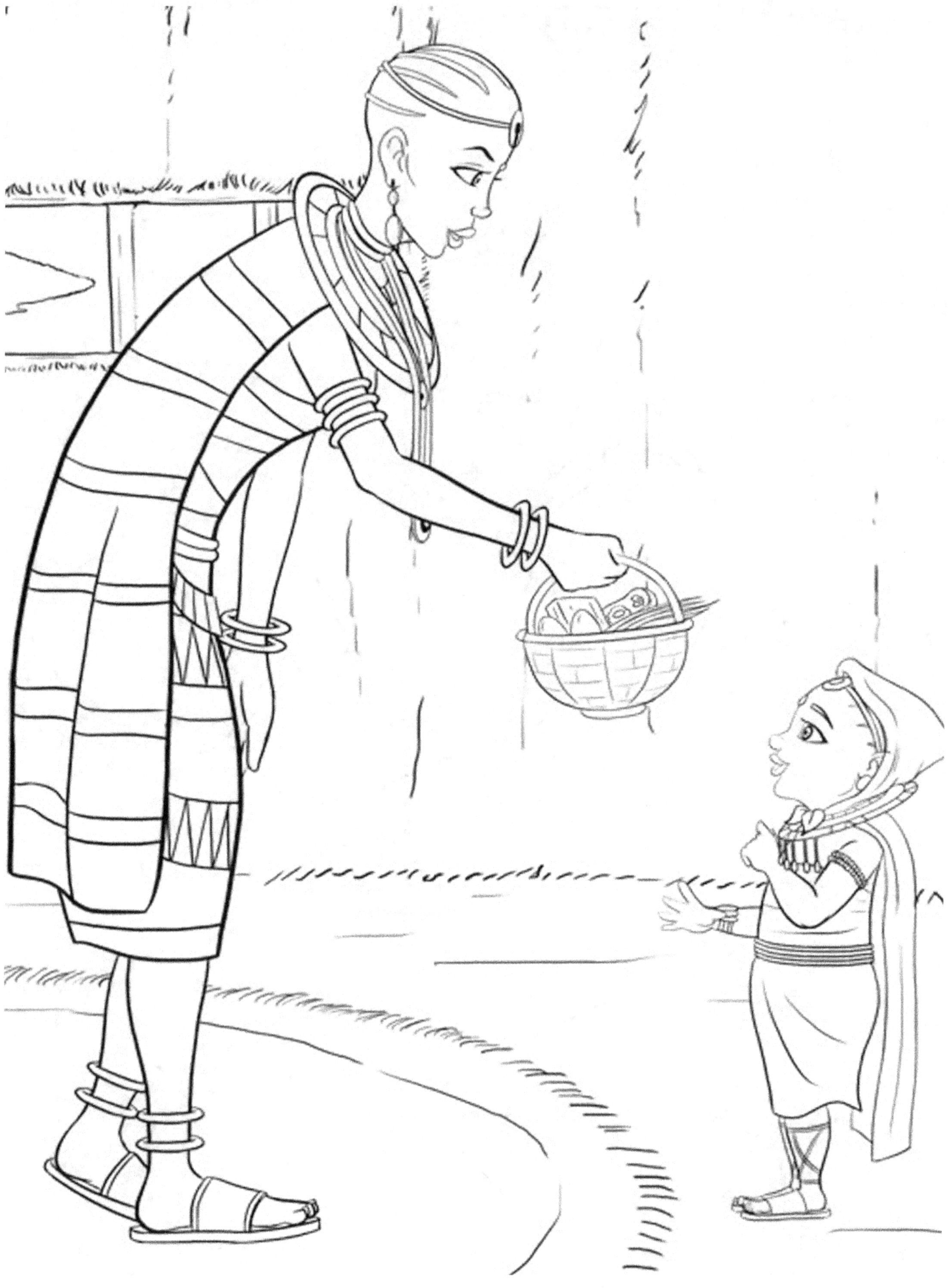

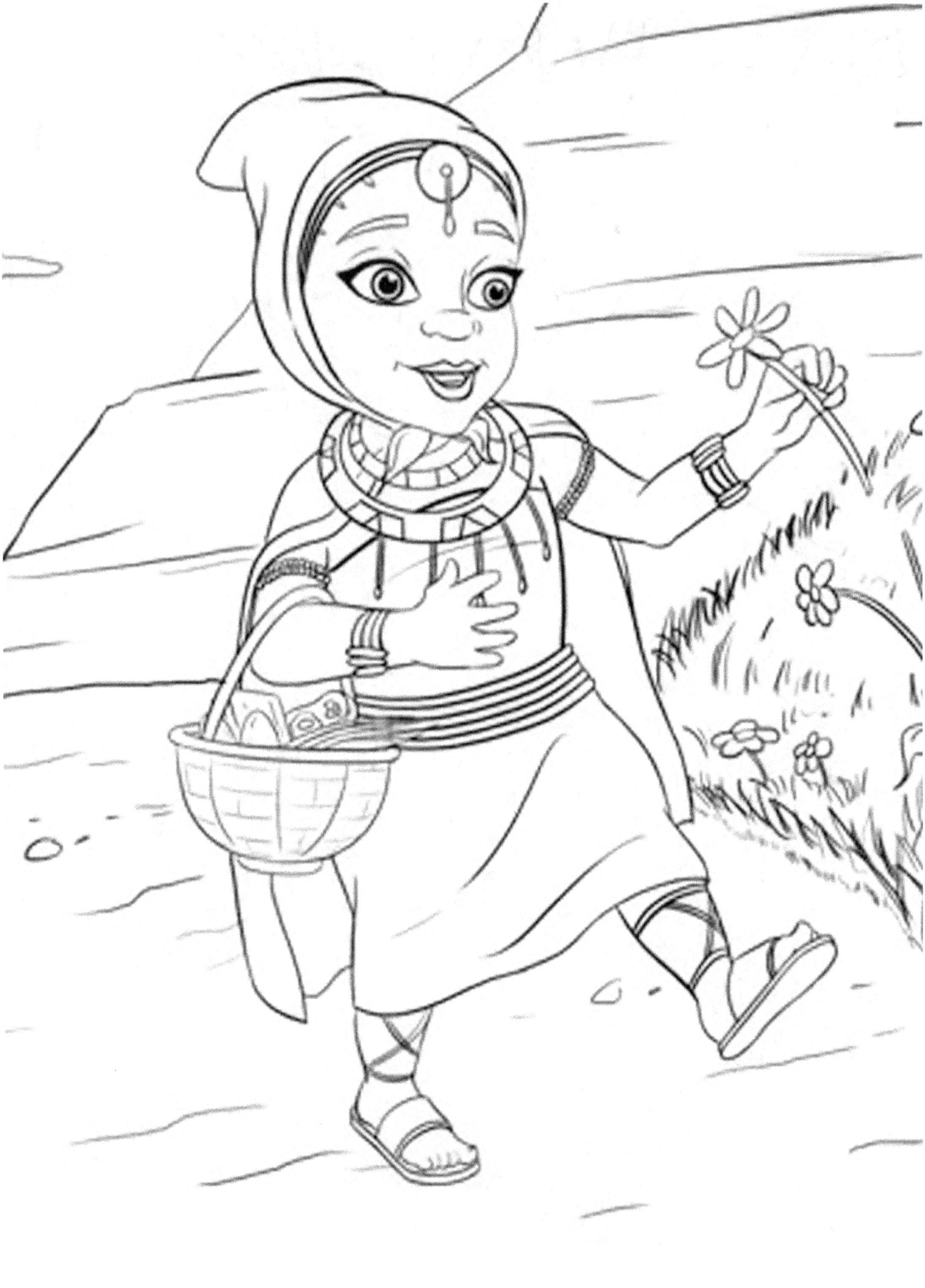

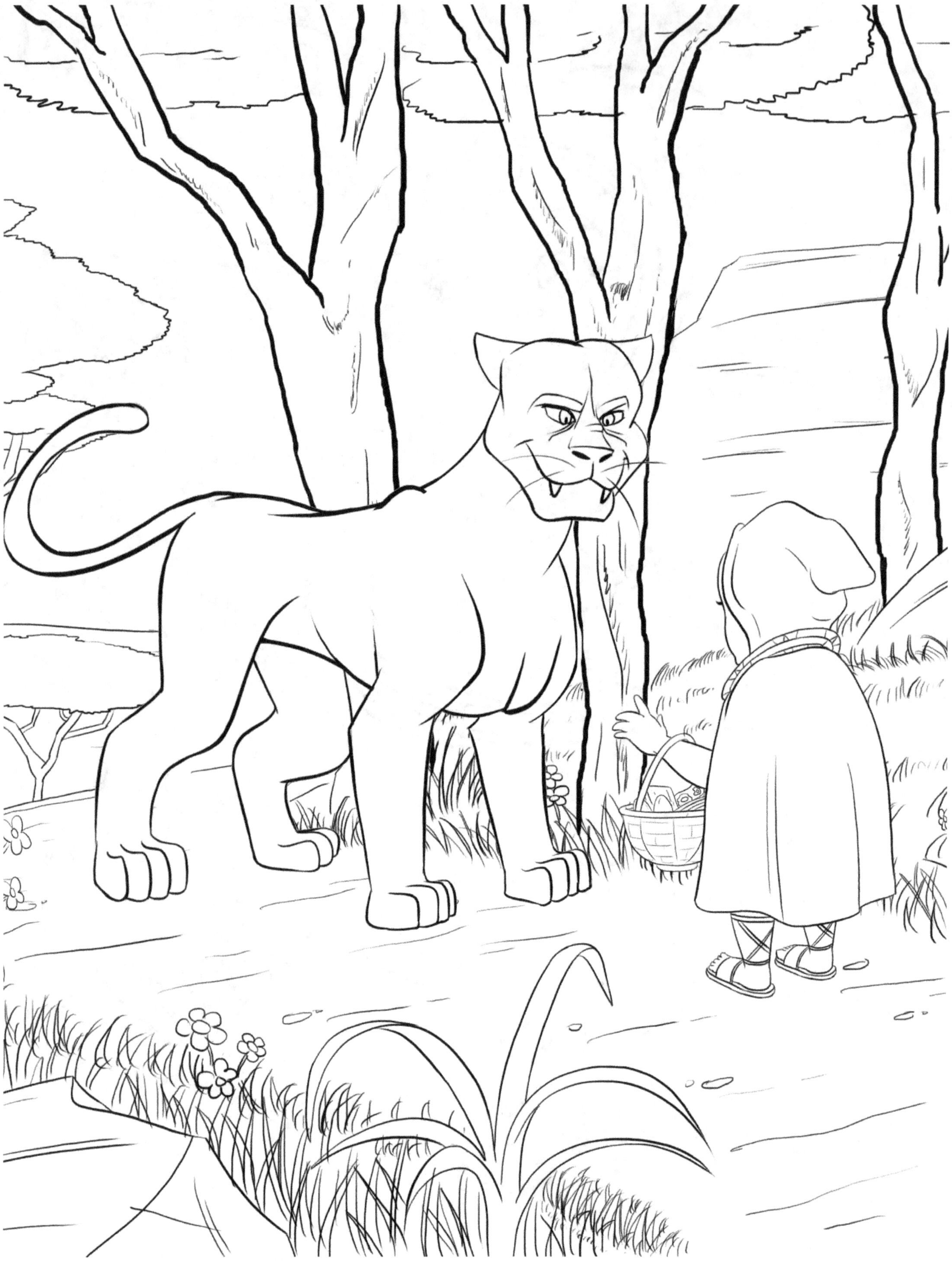

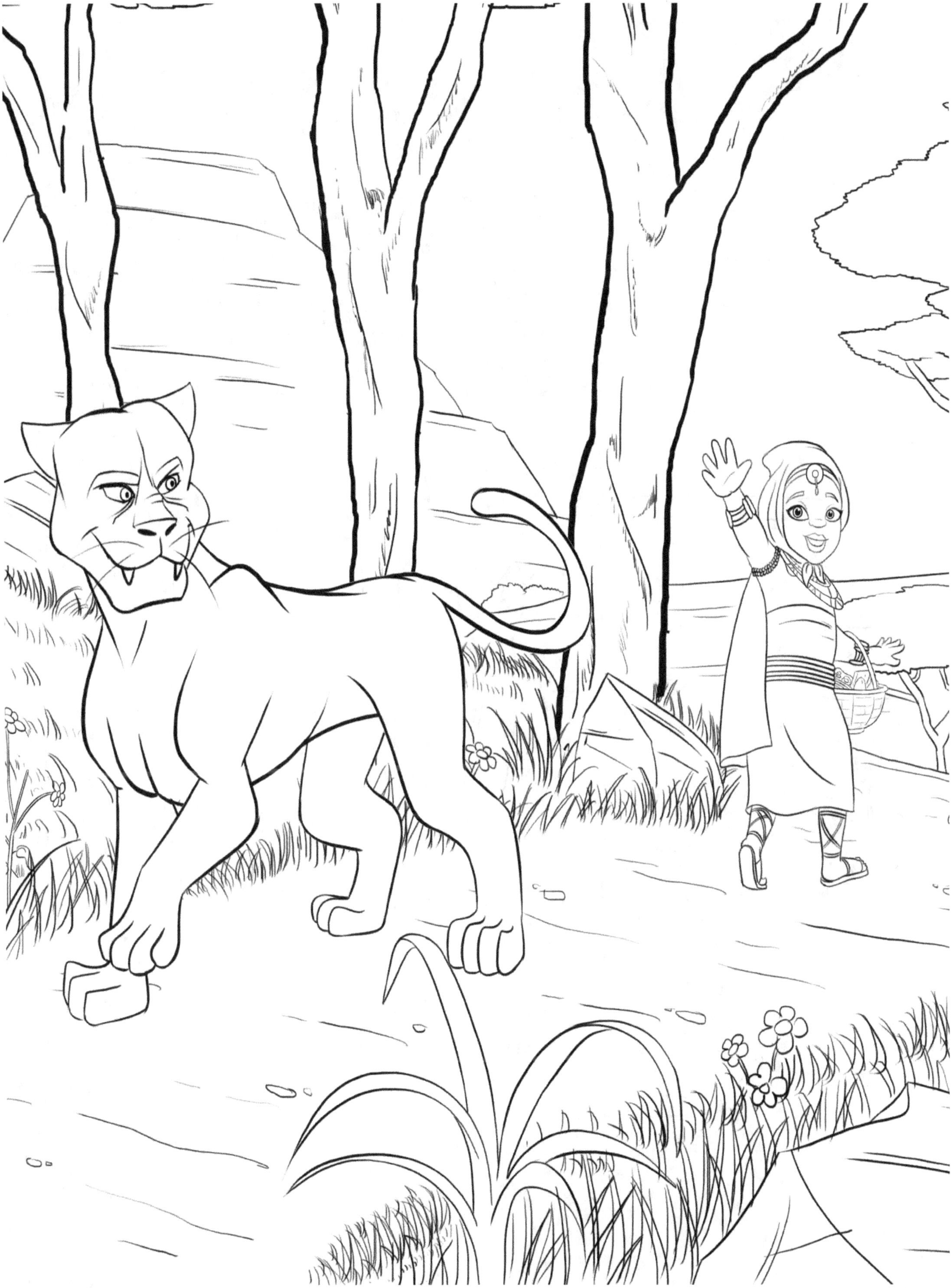

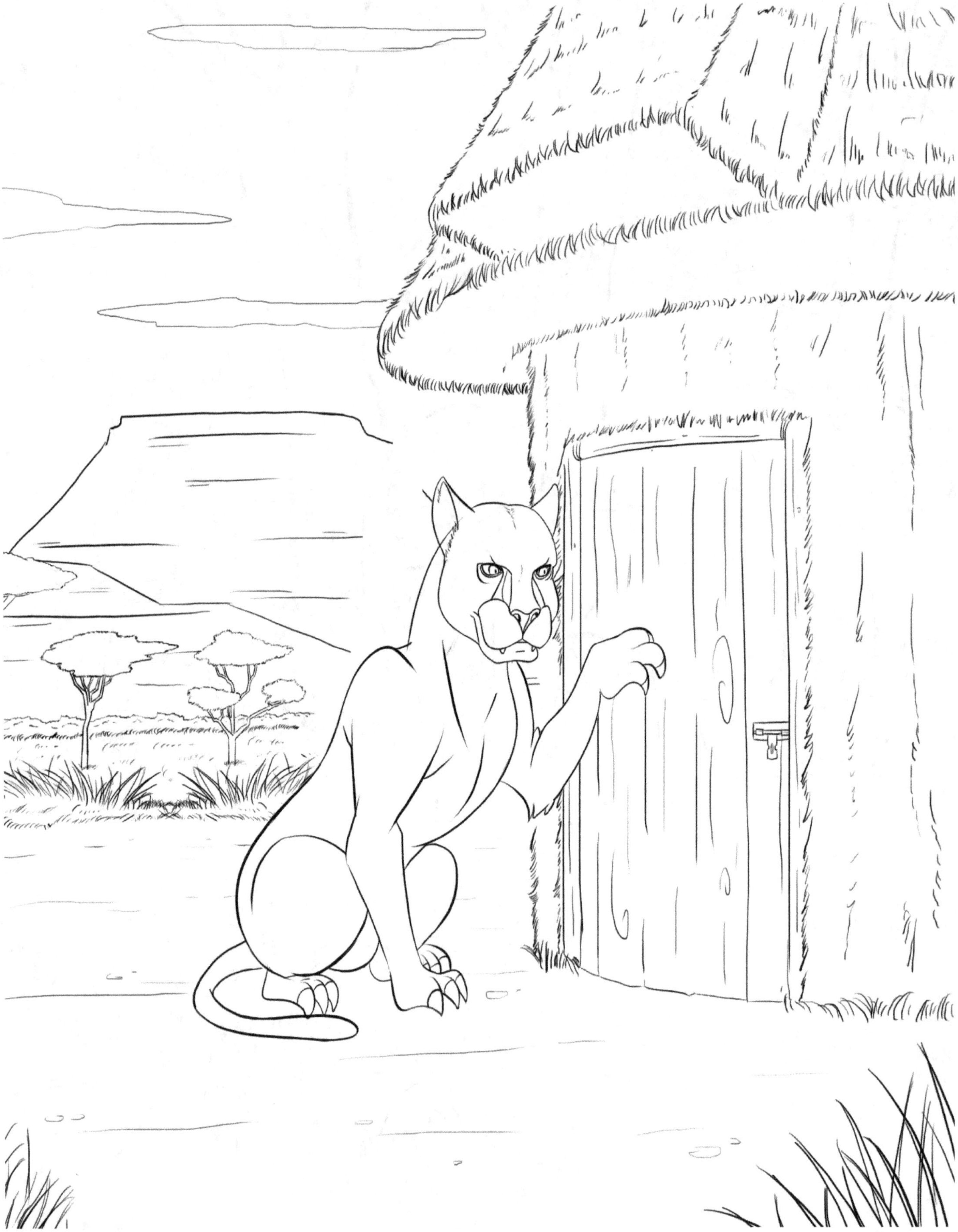

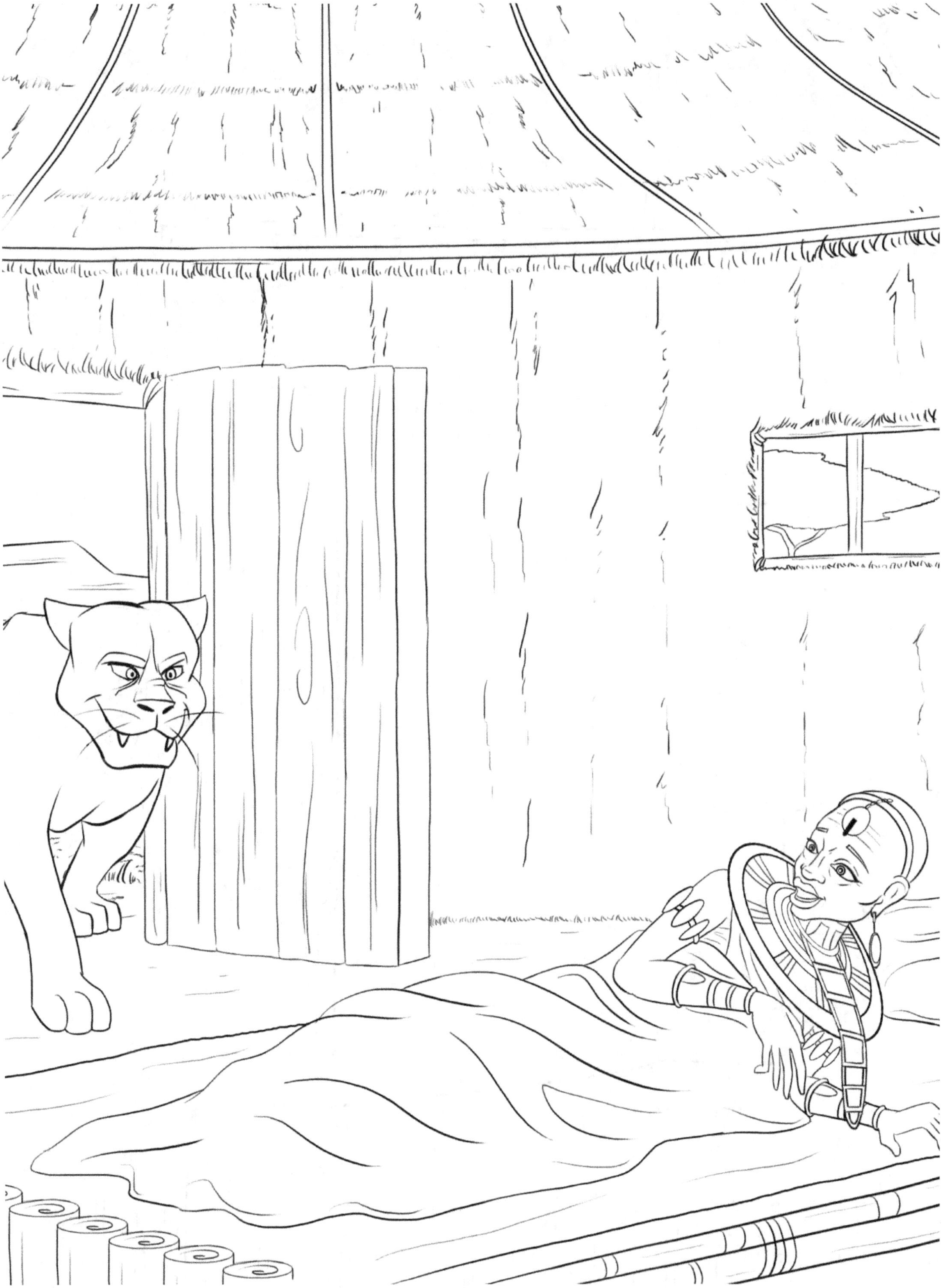

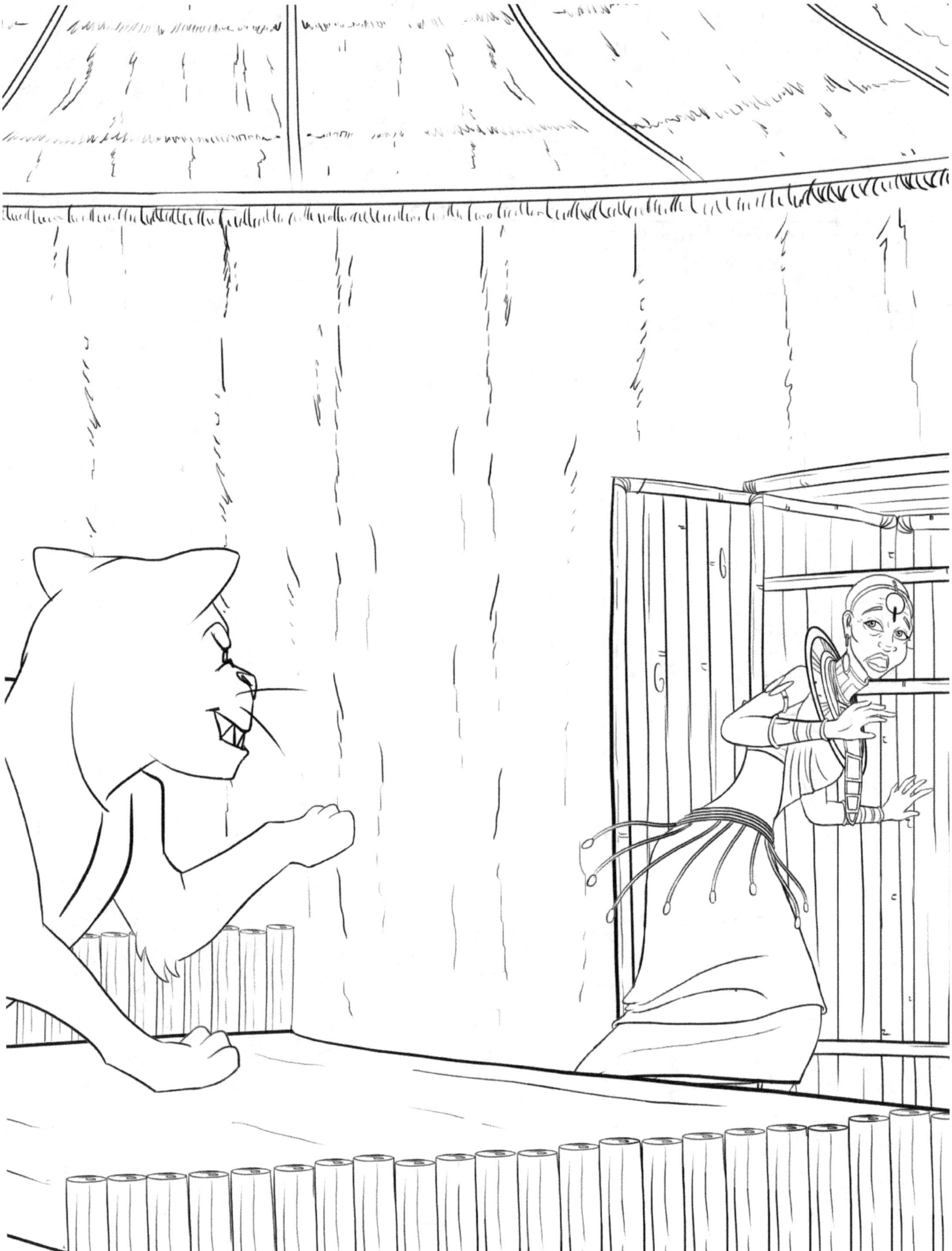

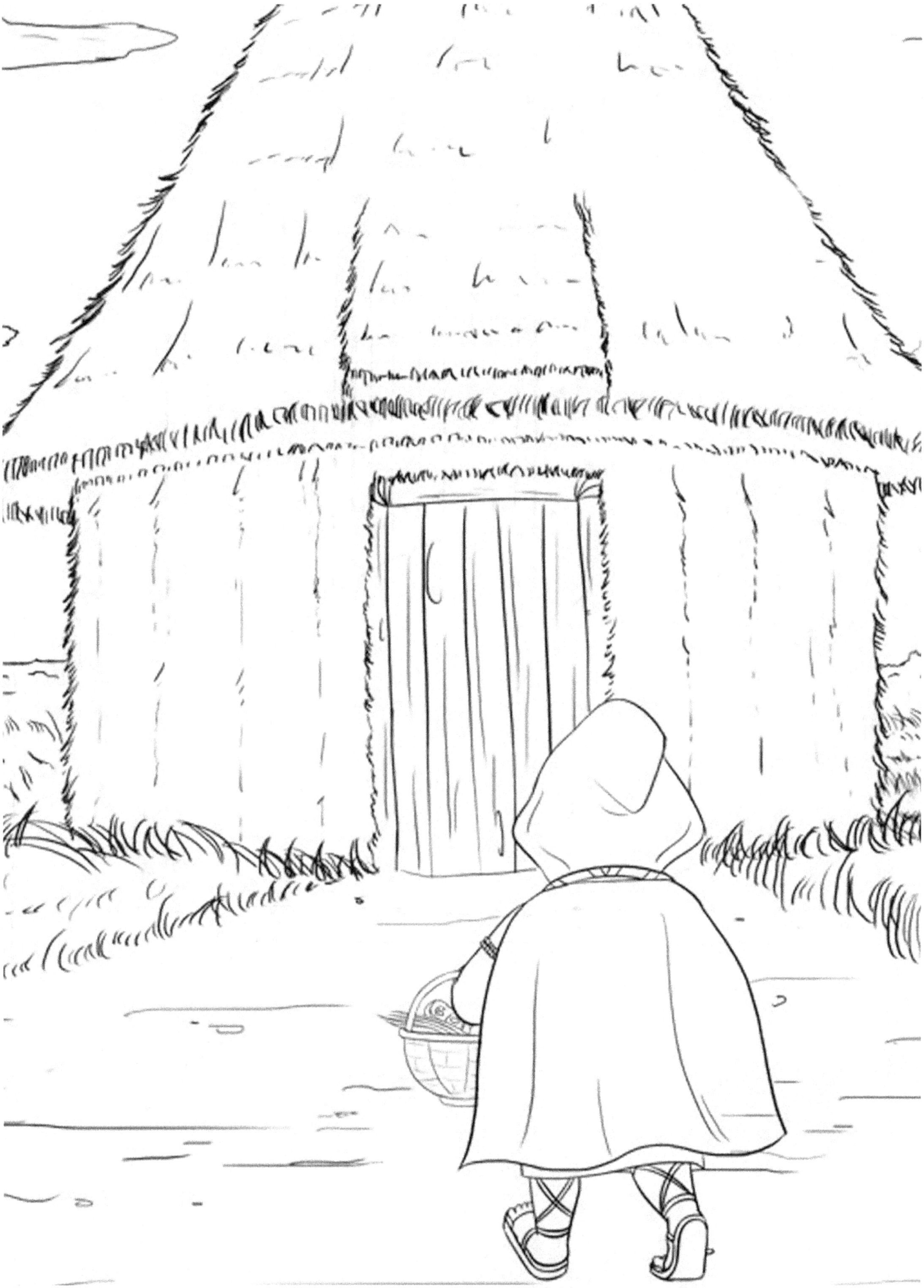

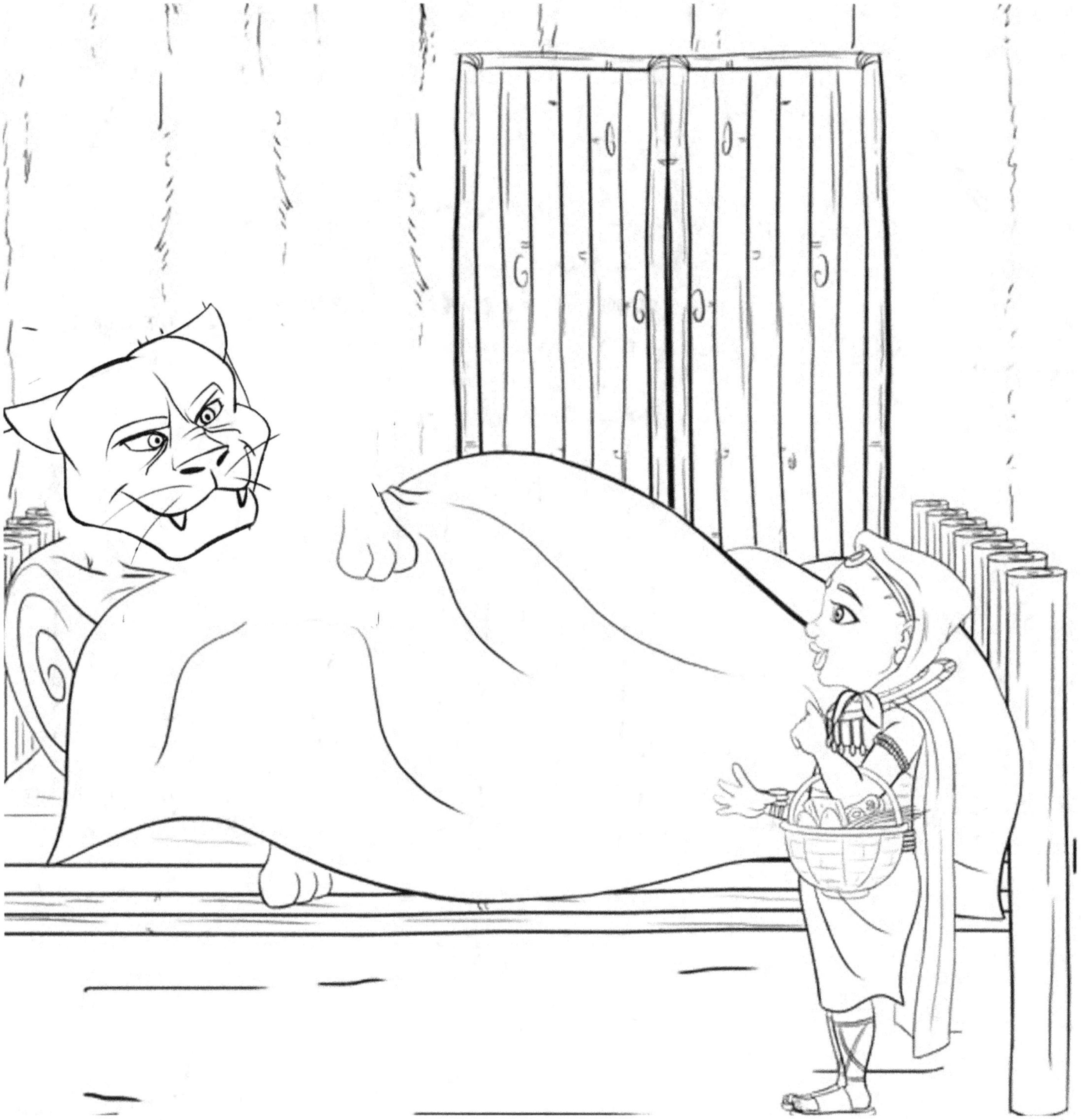

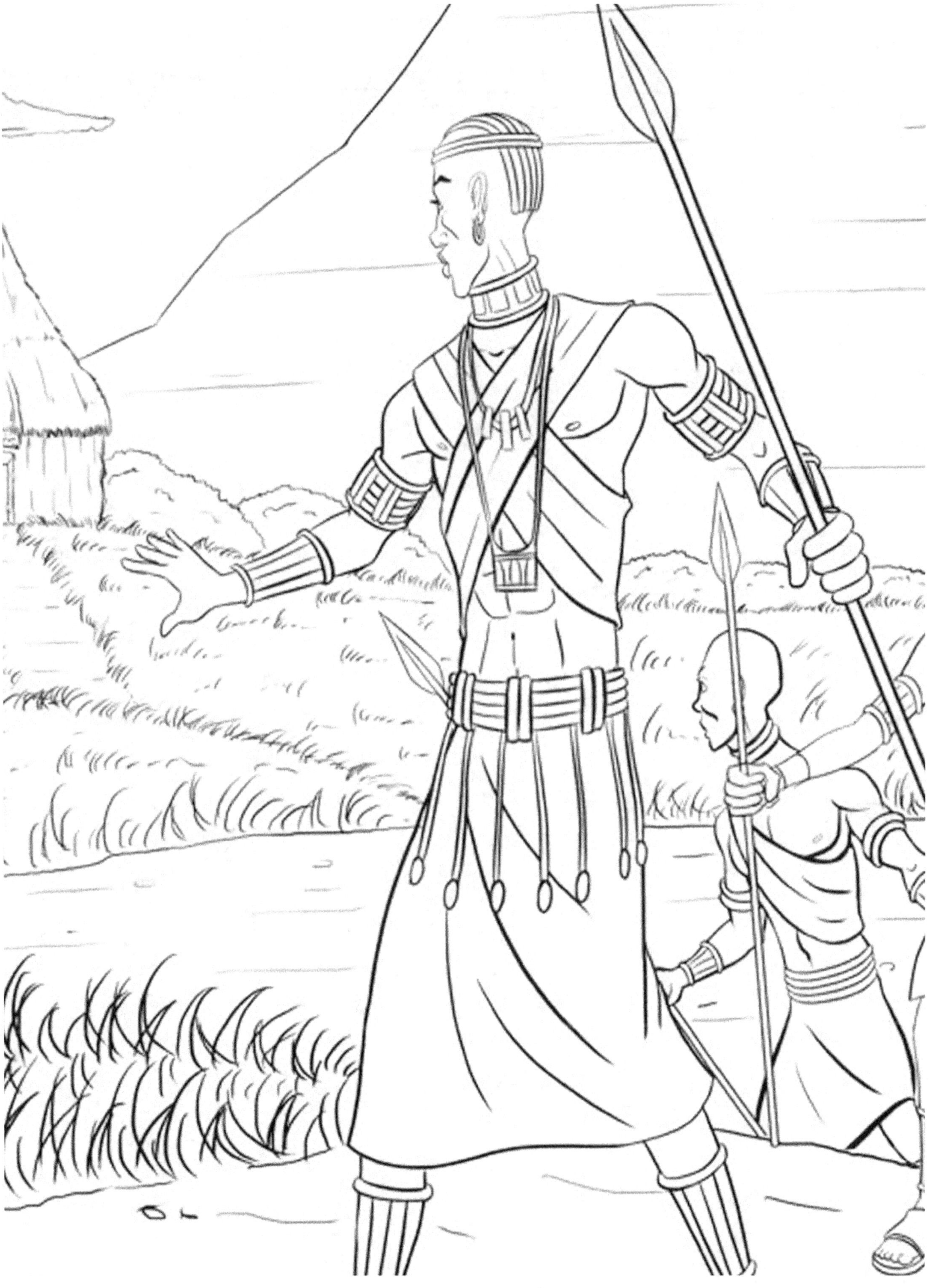

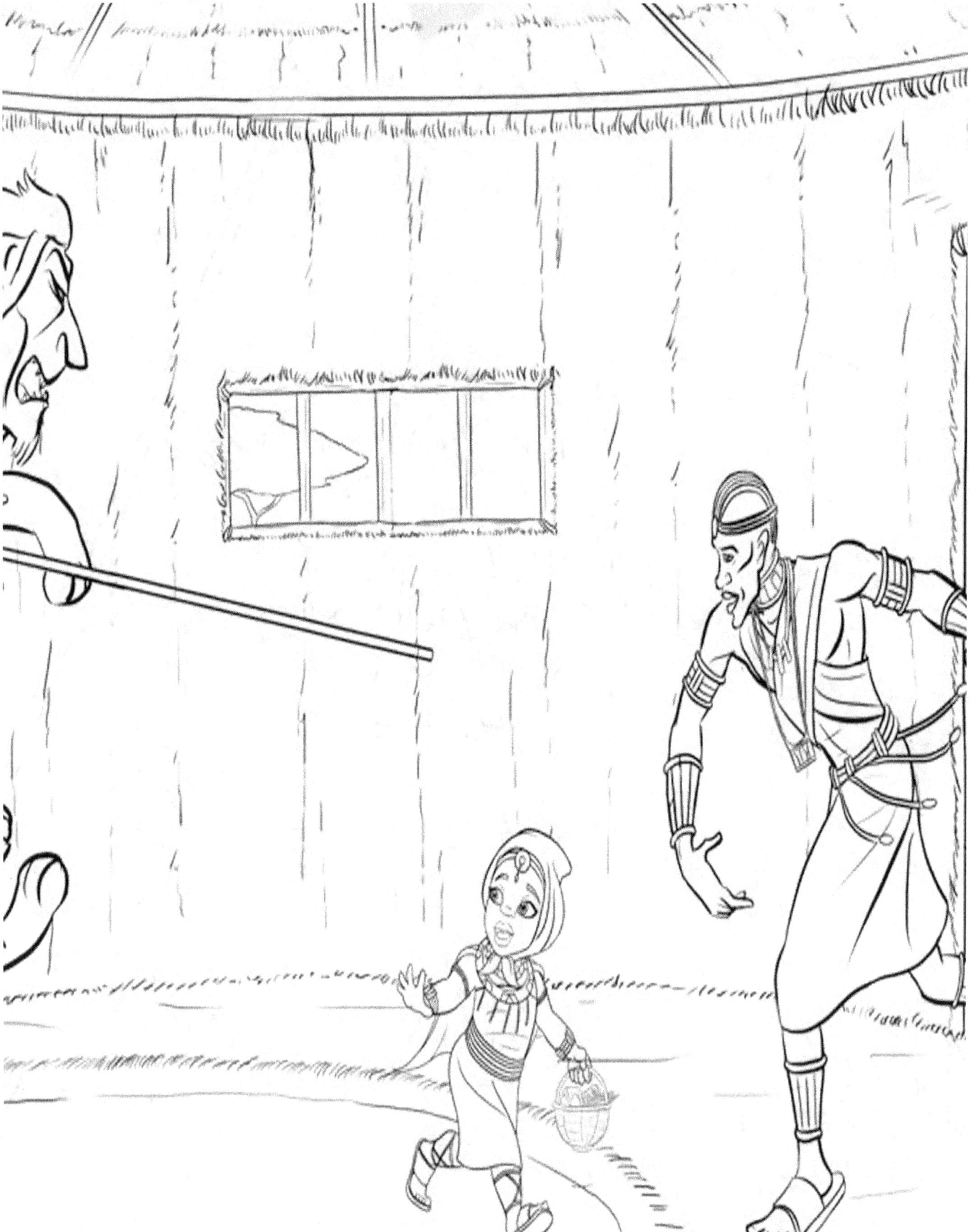

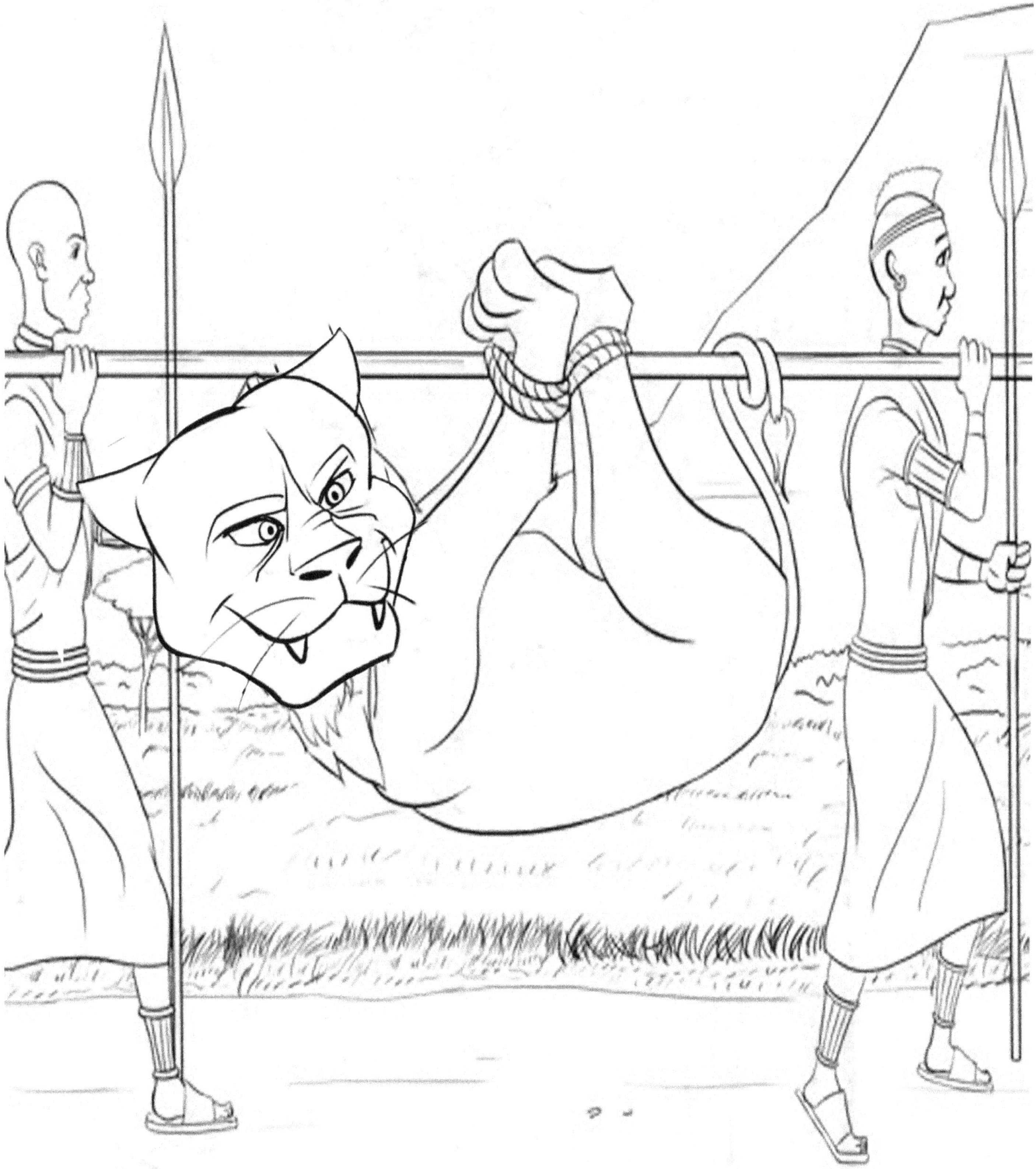

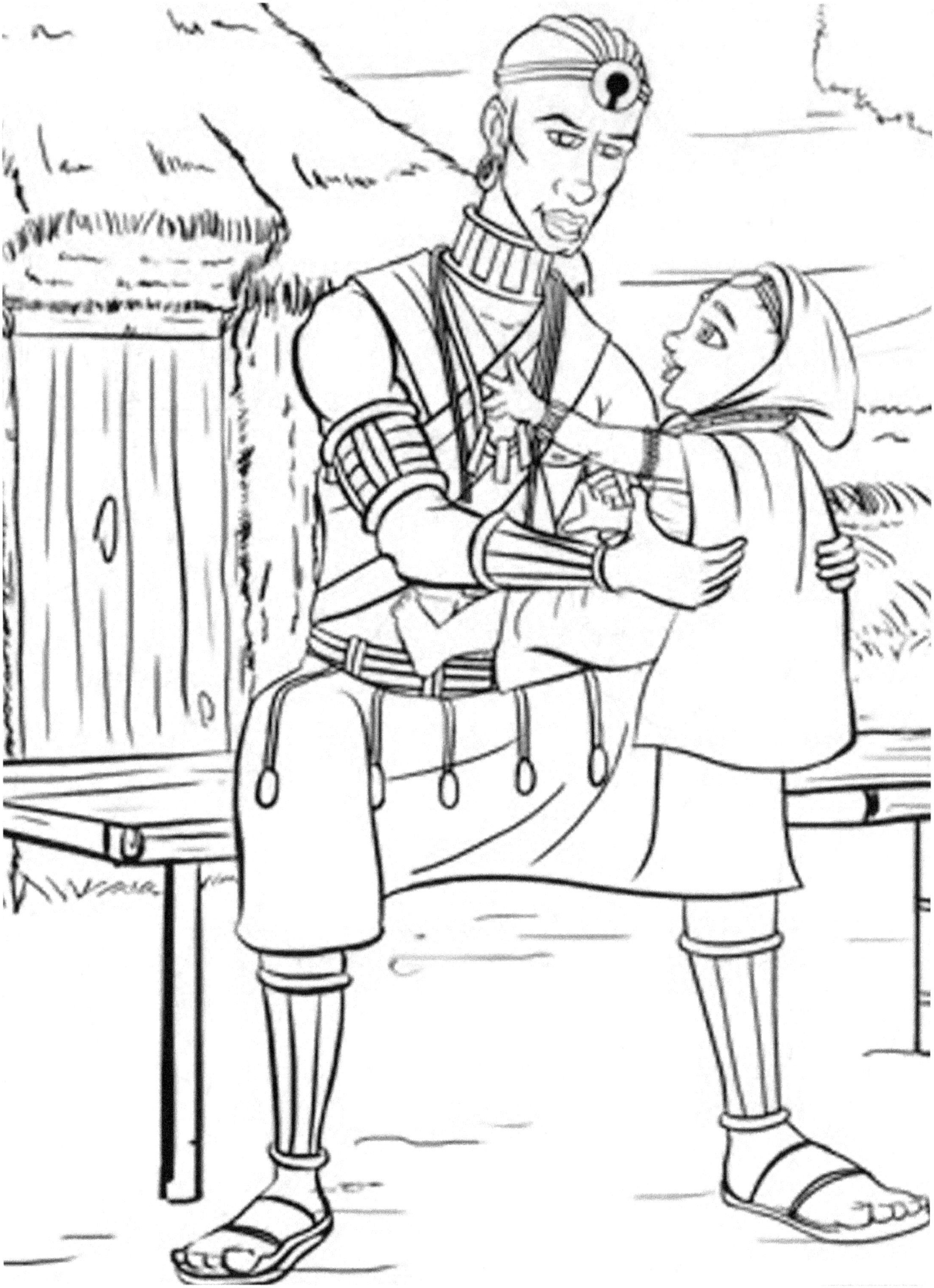

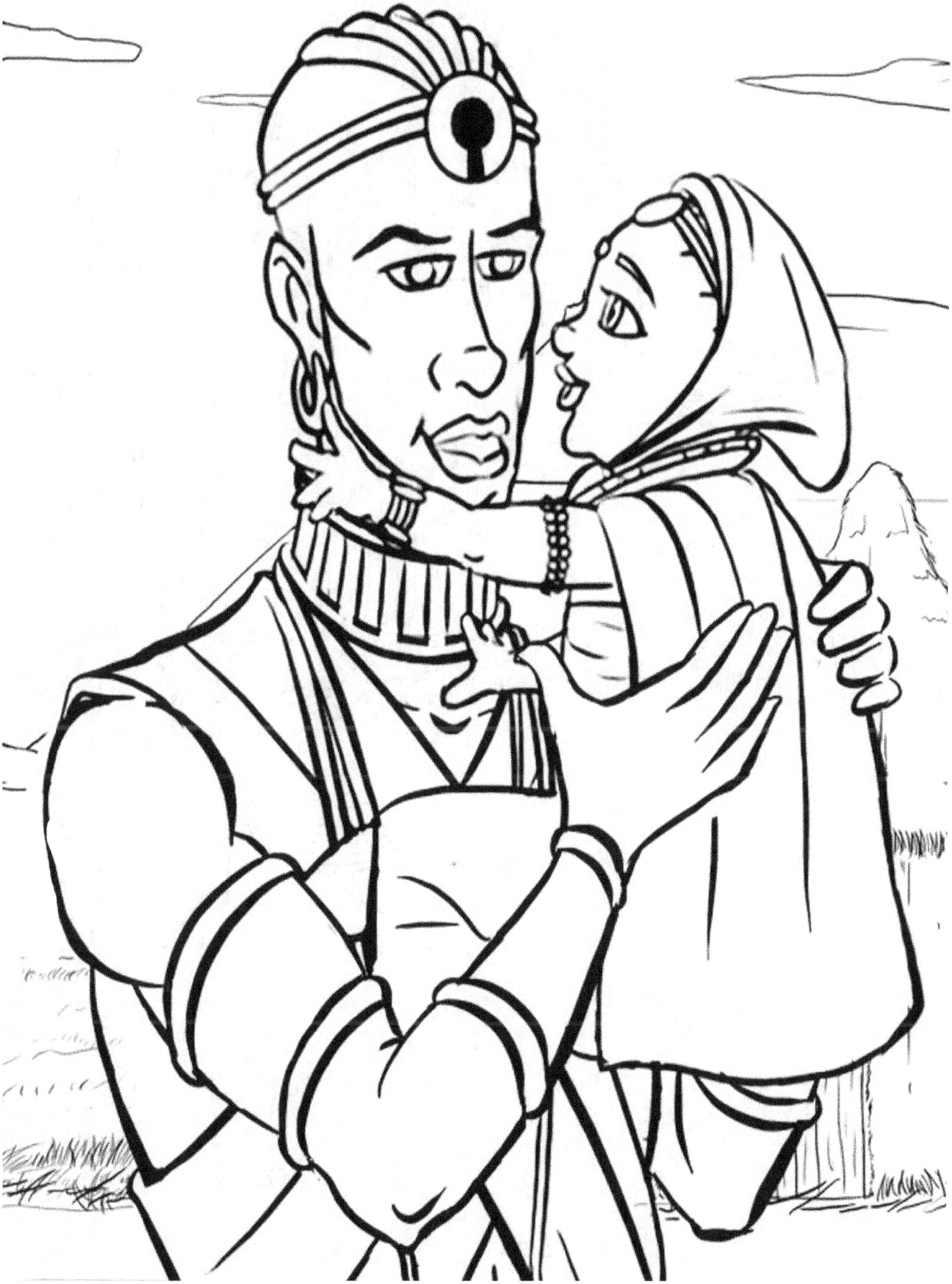

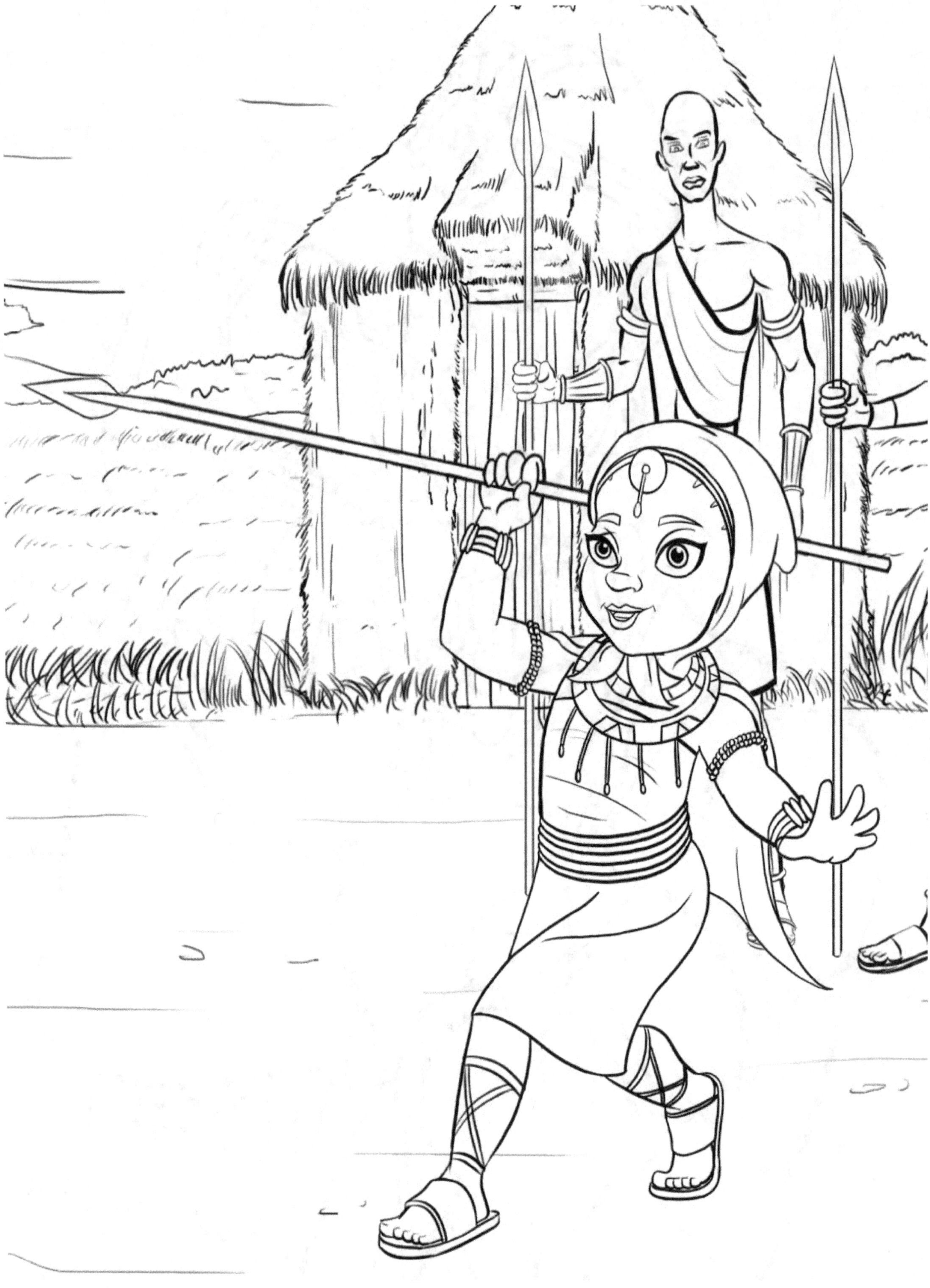

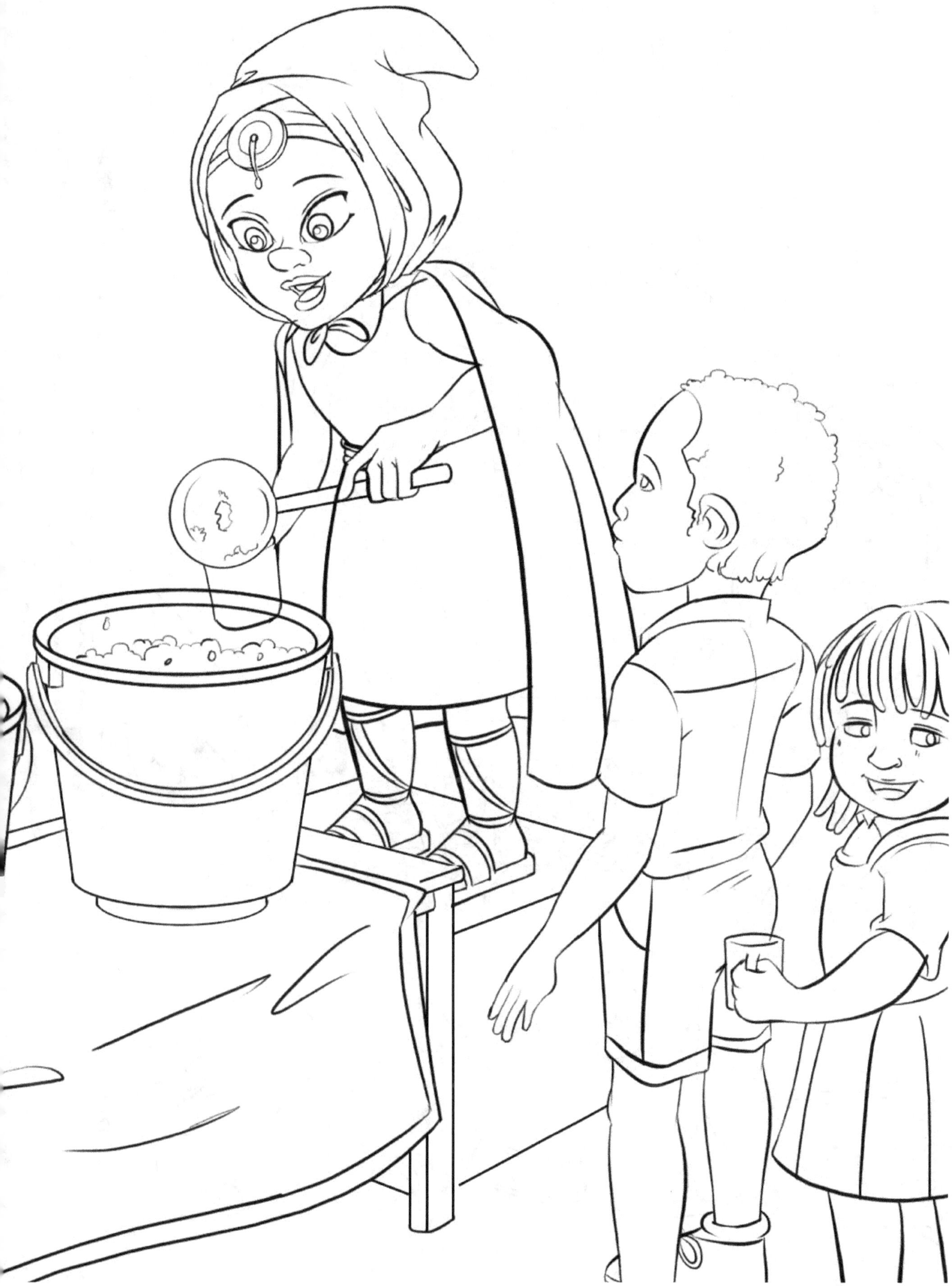

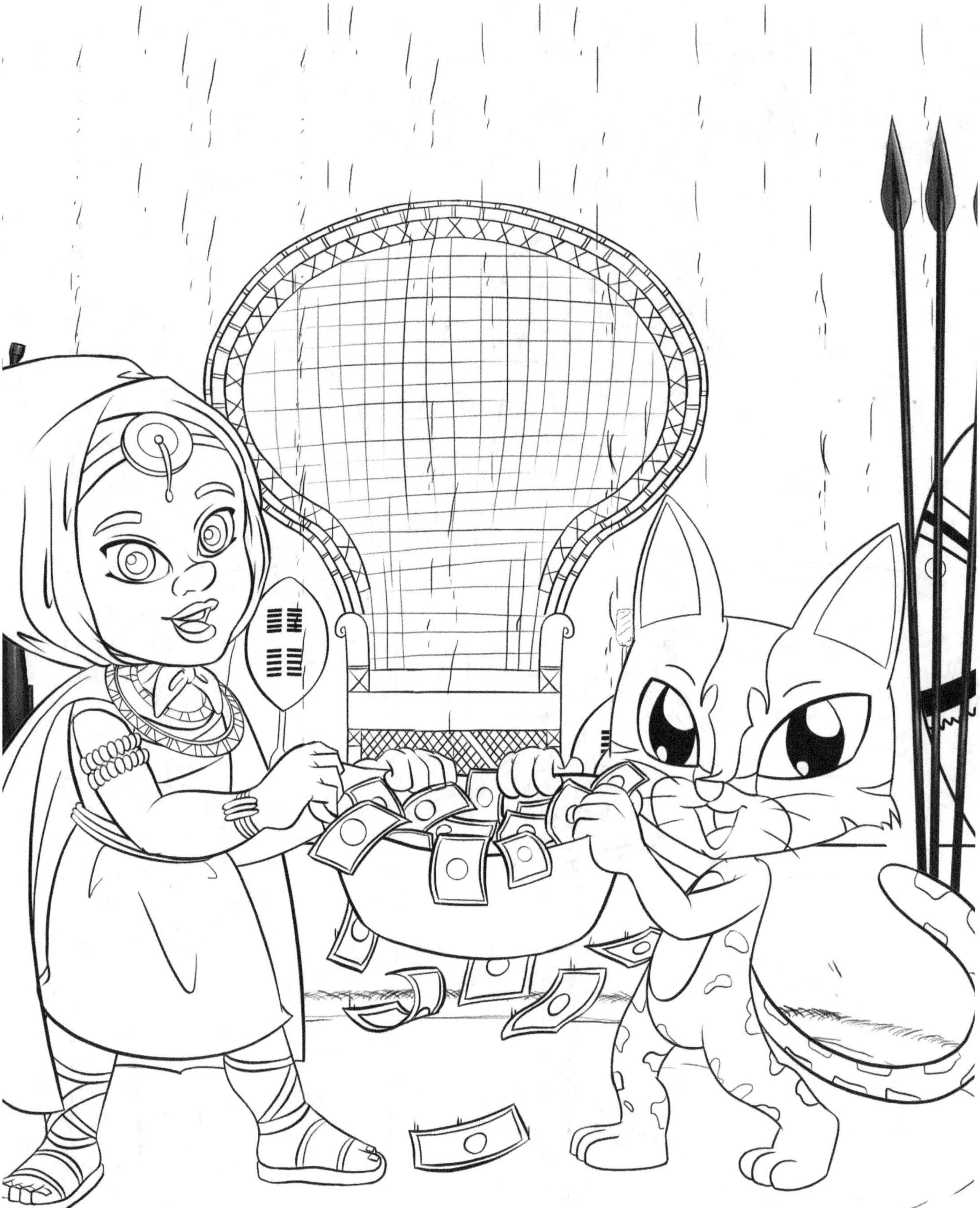

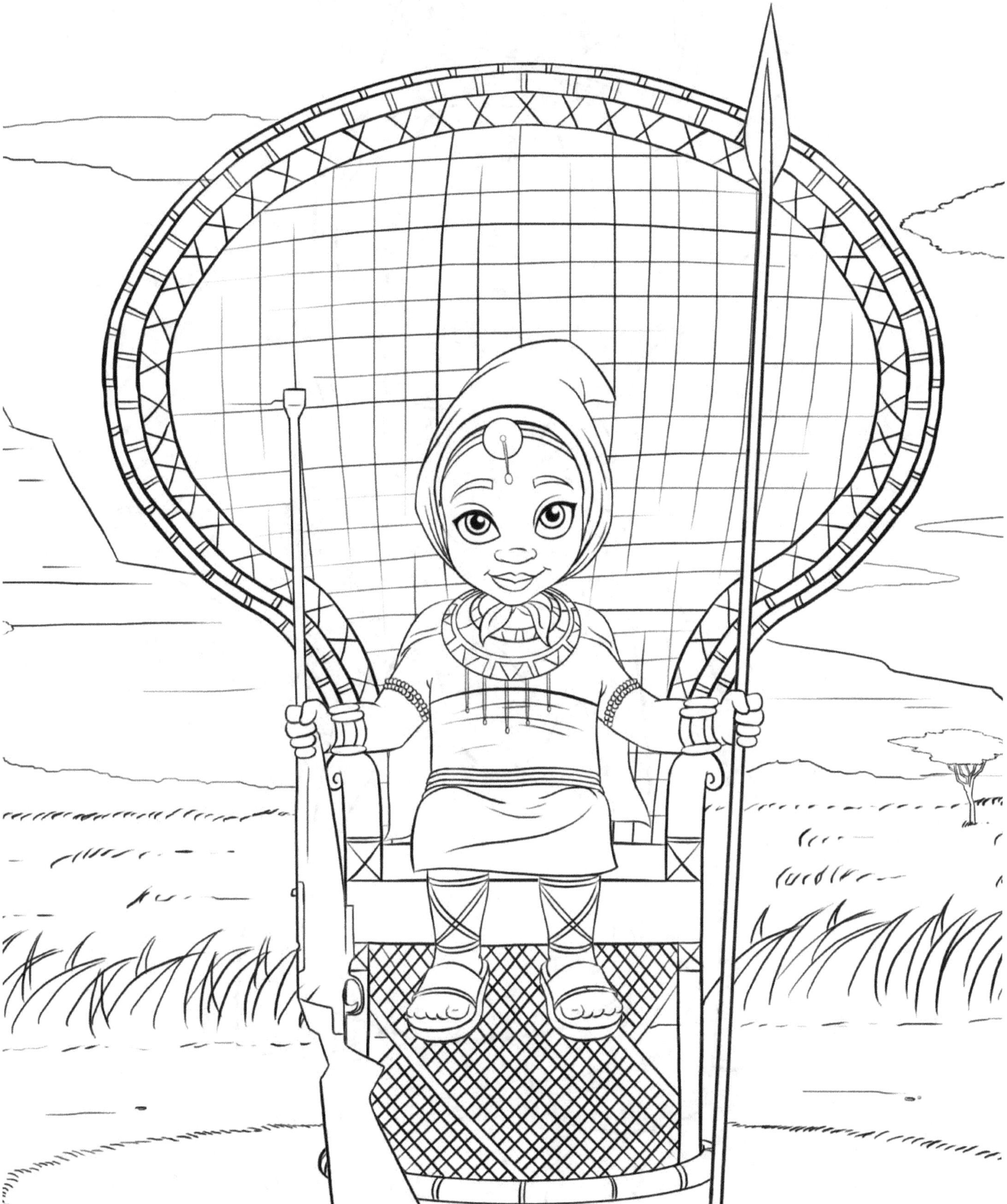

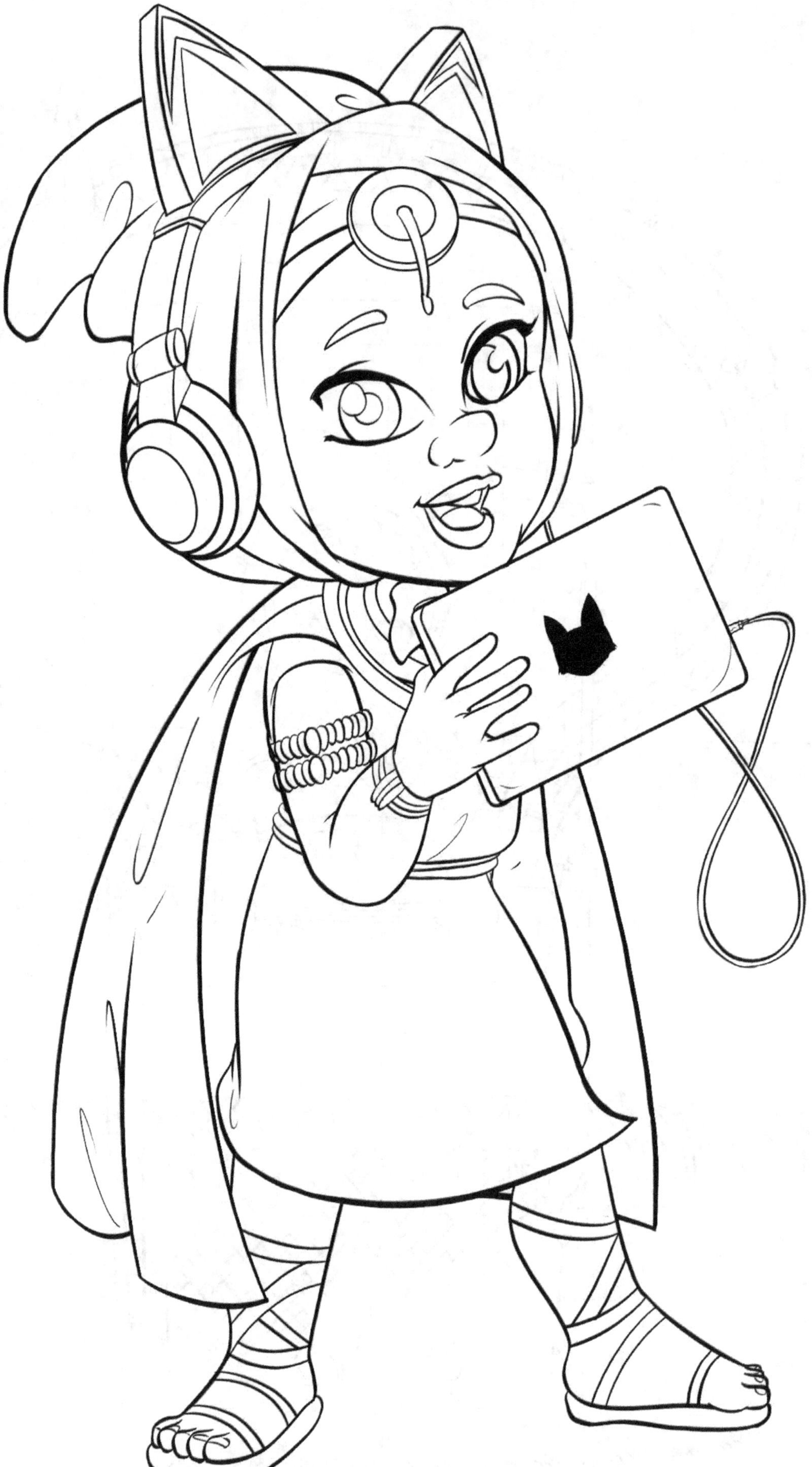

www.ingramcontent.com/pod-product-compliance
Lightning Source LLC
Chambersburg PA
CBHW080631220526
45467CB00011B/3461